Contents

Department of Education and Science
HMI Series: Matters for Discussion 1

Ten Good Schools: A Secondary School Enquiry

A discussion paper by some members of HM Inspectorate of Schools

Majesty's Stationery Office

The publications in this series are intended to stimulate professional
discussion. They are based on HM Inspectors' observation of work
in educational institutions and present their thoughts on some of
the issues involved. The views expressed are those of the authors
and are not necessarily those of the Inspectorate as a whole or of
the Department of Education and Science. It is hoped that they
will promote debate at all levels so that they can be given due weight
when educational developments are being assessed or planned. The
present title (No. 1 in the series) is the outcome of the work of a
team of HM Inspectors led by a Divisional Inspector. Nothing said
is to be construed as implying Government commitment to the
provision of additional resources.

Introduction

This informal small-scale survey of some aspects of the life and work of ten secondary schools was carried out in the summer term of 1975 to test whether generalisations could be made about the factors that contribute to success in secondary education.

In order to select a group of schools to visit, each Division of the inspectorate suggested half a dozen secondary schools which from knowledge acquired in the course of a recent inspection were thought to be 'successful'. 'Success' was interpreted in much the same manner as the Plowden Committee has described the top two categories of primary schools: "In most respects a school of outstanding quality" or "A good school with some outstanding features". Fifty suggestions were put forward and from these ten schools were selected. The sample was so drawn that each region of the country was represented and most types of secondary school, maintained and independent, selective and non-selective, large and small, were included. The visits lasted two to four days and were carried out by small panels, normally comprising the general inspector of the school, two divisional inspectors and two or three subject specialists. Visits were informal, and to secure some rough standardisation of evaluative impressions, panels had an overlapping membership. It is recognised that the analysis of this tiny sample is insufficient foundation in itself to sustain generalisation but the attempt to crystallise what was learnt from observation in ten schools is set in the context of the inspectors' combined experience of very many schools throughout the country.

The traditional freedom of the English educational system puts a responsibility on each school to work out for itself its aims, objectives, methods of teaching and curriculum content. Freedom is of course extensively conditioned by such constraints as public opinion, the expectations of parents, external examination requirements, the limitations imposed by buildings, equipment, staffing and finance, the age, ability and aptitudes of pupils, and, for maintained schools, the policy of the local education authority in organising local provision. Overall, the broad framework is determined by central government.

All teachers have to make day-to-day decisions that will be influenced by their views of ends and means, whether conscious or unconscious, coherent or incoherent. Central and local authorities must make plans in a context in which, more and more, policy will be resource-determined, and questions of priorities and of optimum return for limited expenditure will be inescapable. Their decisions over the whole field of education will, in the last resort, be determined by the general public through the ballot box. The factors which determine the final outcome will be legion. In the schools field, one of the questions central to the debate will be 'what makes a good school.' All parents will have an opinion on the extent to which their child's school matches their expectations, coloured by what they consider best for their child at a particular stage and at a particular moment in time. Professional advisers will also be concerned with the same question but their yardstick will be the more general test of how far a school is succeeding with all its pupils. And in so far as they are called upon for advice over the whole school system, they will be trying to discern in their assessment of schools the principles that lie behind practice, and considering whether the factors which seem to contribute to success in one school could be expected to apply to schools generally, despite the uniqueness of each institution.

The object of this exercise, then, was to look at some aspects of a few secondary schools deemed to be 'successful'; first, to identify characteristics that might be emulated in any school and, secondly, to consider how far such characteristics constitute a common ground of values and objectives shared by schools that differ widely in circumstance. Limits of time and manpower precluded any attempt at comprehensive assessment, and the outcome was in any case intended to be impressionistic and subjective, offering material for discussion. However, to ensure some consistency of approach, visiting panels were asked to give attention to seven aspects in each of the schools. These were:

1. fundamental objectives, and their realisation in relationships, discipline, curricular policies and the personal and social development of the pupils;

2. pastoral care and oversight of academic progress, including administration, organization, communications and the definition of roles and responsibility for staff and pupils;

3. curriculum design and organization (especially appropriateness to the developing needs and capacities of the pupils), content, choice and balance, and planning and co-ordination and critical interest in new ideas on the part of the staff;

4. staffing and quality of work, including clarity of intention and presentation, levels of expectation and standards of response;

5. use of premises and resources, particularly the degree to which the quality of life of the school and the distinctive characteristics of its work are reflected in the environment it creates;

6. links with the local community, including contacts with parents, interaction with the community outside school, and co-operation with other local services;

7. leadership and 'climate'.

Other criteria might have been added or substituted, although these in the event proved central to an understanding and appreciation of all the schools.

Common ground does emerge, and common strengths are discernible in the account of the schools which follows. The evidence suggests that 'success' does not stem merely from the existence of certain structures of organization, teaching patterns or curriculum planning, but is dependent on the spirit and understanding that pervades the life and work of a school, faithfully reflecting its basic objectives. Such objectives would seem to be capable of adoption by any school. The strengths derive above all from the professional skills of the head and staff in creating a well-ordered environment in which learning of all kinds can flourish; within which levels of expectation are at once realistic and demanding, whether in academic performance or in social behaviour; and where functions and responsibilities are clearly defined and accepted.

1   Schools Included in the Survey

Secondary modern schools

Two secondary modern schools, catering for boys and girls between 11 and 16, are included. One is a medium-sized school in a rural area in the North Midlands, built in 1956 and extended in 1964. It has about 600 boys and girls on roll and serves a small town, its surrounding villages and hamlets and some isolated farms. As the selection rate in the area is almost 25 per cent, the school has few academically able children and some of the pupils are socially and culturally deprived. Few proceed to full-time further education and most take up jobs of a practical nature on leaving school, a significant number of boys going into farming or the building industry, and of girls into offices. Nevertheless, the school's results in the Certificate of Secondary Education are distinctly above average for a school of this size and type. The distinctive feature of the school is its success in meeting the needs of its pupils. These are clearly perceived by the headmaster. Academic horizons are limited and so are the pace and scope of the work in comparison with that of urban schools with intakes of higher ability. But the work is steady, straightforward and competent. The headmaster is wise enough to wait until the time is ripe for development and knows that he must have his staff behind him. His priorities are firm: first, to establish a caring community so that the climate shall be 'fit for learning'; and secondly to develop a curriculum that will match the pupils' abilities and interests and be valuable in adult life. Staff enthusiasm and flair have already brought considerable progress in environmental science in which excellent use is made of the immediate surroundings of the school, and in community studies a two-year course of theory and practice for the older pupils has earned them the respect of the locality. As the headmaster of the local primary school said: "Boys whom we had thought of as big unruly 16 year olds we now see as thoughtful, caring, young adults".

The other secondary modern school included is a large mixed school of 1350 in a seaside resort in the south of England. It is noteworthy for its success in establishing itself so rapidly after reorganisation in 1972 which amalgamated what had been separate boys and girls schools. Despite all the remaining problems of the distribution of resources over separated sites and a barely adequate staff ratio of 1 to 20 (particularly in view of the fact that the school operates on a split site), the school runs smoothly, and the turn-out, bearing and response of the pupils testify to the great thought and care given to the reorganisation. The split site has been turned to advantage by establishing the first two years in one building under the deputy headmaster and a senior mistress who are free to establish their own organisation and ethos in ways appropriate to the younger pupils. The headmaster gives a clear strong lead on the objectives of the school and has developed an elaborate system of academic and pastoral care. He is ably supported by a hierarchy of five. Clearly defined responsibilities are conscientiously carried by a hard-working and stable staff. The time that they put in to maintain a consultative system of government through committees and to develop a sense of community with good opportunities for out-of-school activities is most impressive. Careful records are kept and close links established with parents. In the first two years, pupils are organised in ability bands; in the third year, in mixed ability groups; and in the fourth and fifth year partly in mixed ability groups for common-core subjects and partly according to choice of options from no less than 60 possibilities. Standards of work are generally good and examination results above average. This is a large school, recently established, but the professionalism of the staff and the close, structured attention to welfare and to academic progress mitigate the problems of discipline and lack of motivation which may be aggravated in the large school.

Comprehensives in a two-tier system

This type of school is represented by two examples. The first is a medium-sized junior high school catering for 650 boys and girls between the ages of 11 and 14. It is on the outskirts of a large Midlands city in a predominantly middle class area where many parents belong to the professional classes. It was opened in 1968 in fine buildings on a beautiful site with a nature trail in the grounds. Original art work and informative displays make the building interesting; the incorporation of a design centre which offers opportunities for a wide range of activities, and of a resource centre admirably sited and equipped for English and liberal studies, illustrates, the careful educational planning. Here again the success of the school lies in the match between objectives and pupil needs. There is a common curriculum for all with no options, analysed under four headings: languages and social sciences; natural and mathematical sciences; design and cultural; and recreational activities. Block timetabling enables the staff to deploy their forces and vary their methods as they wish, and to work in teams: departmental meetings are timetabled and used to good purpose for evaluation of lessons and courses. Innovation in curriculum organisation and method is thus facilitated but not pursued for its own sake. The overall aim is to reach out to the individual child, but within the framework of a broad, general and liberal education which will serve as a foundation for the more specialised work of the upper school to which they transfer. Standards are good but it is team work rather than virtuoso performance on the part of individual teachers that is the strength of the school. The system of pastoral care is simple and effective, being based upon form tutors who remain responsible for a group of children during their three years in the school. The atmosphere is relaxed but purposeful, and care is taken to ensure that parents thoroughly understand the objectives the school has set itself. The school has a young staff but a headmaster of considerable experience who has reflected deeply on his professional work. He has a firmness of purpose that enables him to resist pressures from articulate and demanding parents if he considers that they are unwise in their ambitions for their children.

The second example is of a mixed comprehensive school for the age range 13 to 18 established in 1969. It is a large 12 form entry school with over a thousand pupils on roll at the beginning of the year, situated in an educational priority area in northern England. Adapted from a former small grammar school, the mixture of old and new buildings provides good accommodation on a pleasant wooded site. The mining town has much unemployment and there are few local opportunities for the academically qualified: only about 10 per cent of the first intake eventually proceeded to higher education. The level of ability in the school's catchment area is recognised as being well below the national average and parental expectations tend to be limited by tradition. The impressive feature of the school is the blend of firmness and imagination which characterises all its work. The broad aim is to provide a sound general education in a well-ordered environment. There is a common core curriculum for all to the age of 16 and a vocational bias is given to some options introduced at the age of 14. The main preoccupation of the headmaster is to help the staff to understand what are the appropriate attitudes towards the less fortunate, the less well-motivated and the less obedient, and to develop curricula which are interesting to the less able. Good standards of work and behaviour are enforced but confrontations and other stress situations are avoided as far as possible. The more severe problems of the school stem from social and family problems rather than from individual revolt and the head finds that he is as much a social worker as a teacher. The school does not advertise itself as a 'community school' but it probably makes as great a contribution to the neighbourhood as other schools so named. Discipline is firm and the standards required are clear but most emphasis is given to example in showing consideration for others. The staff seek to understand and to help without being sentimental or condescending and they give generously of their time out of school. Academic standards are commendable, bearing in mind the larger-than-average proportion of slower pupils that this school has, and the standard of presentation of written work is uniformly high. The requirements of most pupils are met by demanding courses in preparation for external examinations, but the needs of the minority for whom external examinations are inappropriate receive proper attention. For the less able or poorly motivated fifth formers an imaginative course in community study and service replaces the traditional curriculum which is unlikely to provide sufficient stimulus or satisfaction. The small group of pupils with acute social and behavioural problems is catered for separately in a house within the school grounds. The success of the school is attributable to the well-ordered environment established as a result of a consensus of outlook of staff and pupils: there is an absence of tension because all know the objectives and agree upon them. Under the leadership of the headmaster, a stable and exceptionally competent staff keep their work under critical review: they are imaginative and flexible in outlook and willing to adapt, yet clear that professional standards must be maintained. In consequence, the needs of all types of pupil are given proper consideration: the opportunities for the ablest and the interested to develop their talents are good and the nonconformists are treated with a firm sympathy which seeks to help them to achieve the best of which they are capable.

'All-through' comprehensives

Three schools for boys and girls with an age range of 11 to 18 are included in the sample. Two are recently established and relatively small: the third has been in existence for eight years and has a roll of 1500. The first is in a rural town in the Midlands: established in 1970, it has not yet had time to develop a sixth form. The present roll is 770. A large proportion of the pupils travel to school by coach, some for a distance of 12 miles; they have come from 10 contributory primary schools. The catchment area is part urban and part rural and the school population represents a fairly wide cross section of family background. The original building dates from 1953 and three major additions have been made since that date, the latest being most imaginatively and effectively planned through the partnership of architect and staff. Three features of the schools are particularly noteworthy. First, the school sets out to treat the youngsters as individuals and is at pains to know them in their primary schools and in their home settings, and to build up intimate knowledge of them throughout their school careers. Pastoral and academic organisation is interlocking, and formal consultations of year tutors and heads of years as well as of departmental teams are timetabled. A booklet for parents explains the lines of communication and the system by which close oversight and knowledge of each pupil's progress are maintained. Secondly, the headmaster has a clear philosophy and has thought through its application to the particular circumstances of the school. Despite his infectious enthusiasm, however, he counts himself a pragmatist and an executive of the rational, quasi-legal structure he has built up. The staff rate this power-sharing as the most important characteristic of the school and particularly value the freedom given to them—including the most junior—to develop their own ideas. Thirdly, innovatory patterns of organisation and curriculum are firmly based on staff consensus and team work and are evolutionary in character. The school strongly believes in a basic organisation of mixed ability grouping (modified by some limited setting in mathematics, French, and science) which, it is claimed, has brought to the fore the importance of understanding learning difficulties, of linking pastoral care and academic oversight, and of avoiding any streaming of staff. Departmental organisation is strong and has led to initiative in new methods of teaching, integration of subjects, team teaching and extensive out-of-school activities. New courses are carefully explained to parents at meetings, some of which are held in contributory localities. Interesting groupings of subjects have been introduced in the first year in an environmental science course involving science and geography, and in the fourth and fifth years in the humanities, which treats of education for responsibility, for leisure and for careers. Standards throughout the school are good and the experiments in curriculum development produce an atmosphere of freshness and excitement in the learning process.

A second all-through comprehensive, of similar size, is a voluntary aided school which serves a number of generally affluent outer suburbs of London. It was opened in 1969 but already has 102 pupils in the sixth form, including about 30 who are following a non-examination course. It has had the advantage of strong diocesan support and of links with the parishes from which the boys and girls come. Personal relationships in the schools are excellent and are mirrored in the active interest taken by the parents in the school. The full development of the individual, regardless of academic ability, is conceived as being capable of achievement through the school's mixed ability organisation in the first three years, combined with an option system from the fourth year onwards. The provision in the fourth and fifth years and in the sixth form for the full range of ability and aptitude is imaginative: this is one of the factors which has led to the rapid growth of a sixth form, catering for advanced and non-examination courses. Noteworthy features of the curriculum are the amount of time available for all for practical and aesthetic subjects and the special programme of health education taken by all as a core subject in the third, fourth and fifth years. The examination results at ordinary level have been excellent with a high pass rate and a good proportion in the highest grade. CSE results have also been very satisfactory. The organisation for pastoral care and for academic oversight and development is highly structured and efficient, and throughout the school the attitudes of the teachers are determined by respect for the individual rights of the pupils. The children respond well and work hard; the staff are well led and give of their best; the objectives of intellectual and spiritual development are clearly promulgated and in its short existence the school has made substantial progress towards traditional goals.

The third comprehensive school catering for boys and girls from 11 to 18 has been in existence longer (it was opened in 1967) and is very much larger, with 1500 on roll. Unlike the other examples it is essentially a neighbourhood school serving a not very prosperous area on the outskirts of a great industrial city in the north of England. It is situated in pleasant surroundings but as local engineering industries have declined the proportion of skilled artisans employed in the area has dwindled and that of semi-skilled and unskilled workers has increased. Despite the change in fortune of the district this neighbourhood school has gone from strength to strength, and though its intake remains predominantly local it is significant that a good number of parents in other parts of the city now select this school as their first choice. It would be difficult to single out for particular appraisal any one aspect of the school. Indeed the school's strength and character seem largely to lie in the overall evenness of its virtues: the commonsense, goodwill, decency, moderation, patience and tolerance that control everyone's actions. If nothing hits the heights spectacularly, nothing approaches anywhere near the depths; and the whole commands great respect and considerable admiration. Though the educational aims have not been formalised or enshrined in a document they are known and accepted by the staff and pupils and provide a firm but unobtrusive policy which informs and motivates the administrative, academic and pastoral life of the school. The underlying philosophy is based on a respect for the individual and for his contribution to the community as a whole. The main aims may be summarised as the development of self-respect, respect for others and for other living things, respect for the things of the mind and respect for property. These basic aims are actively supported by a consensus of attitudes and behaviour within the framework of a serene community. The simple system whereby this large school is divided into lower, middle and upper sections creates smaller, more homogeneous age-groups with which the pupils can identify and within which the broad educational aims can operate more obviously. Interestingly, the educational objectives have been translated into traditional subject terms but the pupils accept that this is what school is all about and parental expectations and the needs of the community reinforce this general agreement. Discipline is excellent and is based on mutual trust and respect. Corporal punishment is used on those who harm the community by violence or bullying and is seen as a necessary evil. In general, standards of behaviour and of effort are uniformly high and there is a surprising evenness in the quality of the teaching across the whole curriculum as well as within the separate departments. Examination results in GCE, Ordinary level, and CSE are very creditable in most subjects (two only being poor) and those capable of advanced work who stay on at school have done extremely well. Indeed the development of a sixth form of 85 reflects great credit on the school since very few pupils come from homes where extended education is taken for granted.

Although it is difficult to isolate the factors which make for success in this school one observable feature in both the social and academic life is the high level of participation of the staff. This applies equally to the probationers, who have been very numerous in the past few years: each has a tutor responsible for induction and welfare and, like the new pupil, they quickly learn the outlook of the school. It is part of the remarkable character of the school that it can turn what might in many circumstances have been a disadvantage into a strength. One teacher aptly summed up the sources of the school's strength as 'leadership, hard work and flexibility, to which he might well have added 'the corporate concern of the community for its members'.

Selective schools

Two examples are included, both ancient foundations and both for boys only. One is a direct grant day school, the other a day and boarding independent school.

The direct grant school is in a city in the south west of England. As a day school it serves an extensive local catchment area. The inclusion of a few choristers means that some entrants are aged 10. With selective intake average ability is high, and more than a quarter of the 400 on roll are in the sixth form. Although an avowedly academic school running on traditional lines it seeks to provide, within the limits of its facilities (there is no craft workshop), a balanced and liberal education suited to the individual's needs, desires and abilities. It is sufficiently small and homogeneous to make very effective provision for pastoral care, academic oversight and staff development without elaborate organisation. The progress, welfare and school career of every pupil is intimately known and carefully fostered. The range of home background is comprehensive but career objectives are, in general, uniformly academic and professional. Such ambitions are well catered for: the ability of the boys is matched by the ability of the staff so that boys are challenged and extended: examination results are excellent and many proceed to higher education with high grades. It is not surprising that though this is a small school the classics flourish. There is a genuine regard for and understanding of scholarship under leadership which is dynamic, committed, cultured and intelligent. What is noteworthy is the readiness to pursue the discipline of the traditional subjects in new ways. Such is the purpose of the course in outdoor education, which combines local studies with training in outdoor pursuits, or of the opportunity (for a few) to put on tour two Shakespeare plays, and their own street plays in a seaside town, and to achieve real excellence in performance. It is also noteworthy that though pupils are encouraged to be academically ambitious and not to be content with minimum qualifications, subject learning in the sixth form is firmly placed in the context of liberal understanding and social sympathy through a comprehensive programme of general studies.

At the independent school chosen, three forms enter at 11, of which about two-thirds are selected by the County according to its normal procedures and one-third are fee payers selected via the school's own examination. There is a further entry of two forms of fee payers at the age of 13, selected on the basis of the Common Entrance Examination. A further 30 boys, of whom 20 are from overseas, join an international centre, which is an exclusively sixth-form boarding house. The total roll is 833 of whom 285 are in the sixth form; a quarter of the school are boarders. The school offers what might be termed a traditional grammar school curriculum in which Latin is compulsory; but it is possible to study three sciences and two languages or three languages and two sciences. Undue early specialisation is avoided, however, by making creative studies a core subject until the end of the fourth year and by offering wide opportunities on two afternoons a week for 'club' and other practical activities. The resources of the school are numerous and impressive, and include a drama room and theatre; a concert hall and music room; a technical activities centre; an audio-visual language centre; a reprographic unit; a television studio used by pupils and teachers for producing tailor-made study kits; a wide range of sporting and boarding facilities; and a new library complex which is nearing completion. The pupil/staff ratio is just over 13 to 1, but class sizes in the main school average 27 pupils, demonstrating the expensiveness in man-power of a large and diversified sixth form, of the incidence of boarding duties, and of responsibilities for clubs and societies.

With an established reputation, a highly selective entry and a privileged position as regards physical and teaching resources it is to be expected that overall standards would be high and examination successes at university level outstanding. What is interesting is that the school does not rest content with its pioneer efforts in project technology. Experiments in the curriculum are not only the result of the influence of a visiting 'Fellow' (currently concerned with developing resource materials on slide, film and videotape for the classroom) but spring from the work of departments which pool their ideas on curriculum development, reappraise their methods and seek new forms of overlap with other subjects. Regular attendance at short courses is a feature of staff training and departments keep well abreast of contemporary thought in their subject areas. The results of such lively professional interest are to be seen in such things as the introduction of Mode 3 syllabuses in English at both ordinary and advanced levels, the pupil exchange scheme with a French school, and well established integrated courses in the junior school. It is also of interest that the school does not seek to mould the boys in its own image: apart from the serious concern for the pastoral care of all pupils, whether day boys or boarders, and for careers education (even though the majority proceed to universities, the professions or parental firms), this concern for the individual extends to the curriculum, and it is noteworthy that CSE groups exist in French and German, for example. Nonetheless, the outstanding characteristic of the school remains its broad aim of developing self-discipline and of "encouraging self-expression and self-realisation through creative activity".

A special school

The last school included in the sample is a selective school of a different kind. This is a special school for educationally subnormal children [ESN(M)] in a small country town in a rural area of the Midlands. Of the 82 on roll, 65 are girls, of whom 56 are weekly boarders. The 17 boys are in the lowest age group and are all day boarders. The school was opened in 1954 under its present headmistress, who is now assisted by nine teachers qualified in teaching the handicapped.

The leadership of the headmistress is the determining factor in the success of this school. Her enthusiasm, administrative ability, professional skill and long experience are shared with a carefully chosen staff. In consequence there is a team approach, and regular consultation among teachers and housemothers contributes much to the understanding support given to each individual pupil. In a handout prepared for the staff the headmistress writes, "Attainment is almost wholly dependent on the *experience* which both the individual teacher and the school as a whole can give to this type of child", and her basic aim is to ensure that the children have the kinds of experiences which breed confidence and self respect and promote learning. Classification in the school is based on social development rather than on chronological age; some groups have a wide age range but the pupils are compatible within the group in terms of sociability. The pupils are helped to understand the ends in view, to contribute to the planning of the curriculum, to make choices and decisions and to assess their own efforts.

The curriculum is primarily designed to stimulate interest in the immediate environment of the school and its locality; through the experiences that arise the pupils are led to realise the need to communicate and to calculate. Aesthetic experience is stressed and the children find enjoyment and enrichment in movement, art and craft and music. The quality of the children's pictures and models displayed in classrooms and corridors testifies to the satisfaction and success that they experience. Both boys and girls follow a practical course in home economics and the two men recently appointed to the staff are introducing craft activities traditional for boys which will be shared by both sexes. As the children grow older, the curriculum becomes more outward looking. First class use is made of the Duke of Edinburgh Award scheme, adapted to the aims and objectives of the school, and through the opportunities for community service that this provides, close links are developed with the neighbourhood. Work experience is also well planned and integrated with the programme for the last two years of school. Throughout, the teaching is characterised by careful preparation, clear understanding of individual needs and a warmth and patient encouragement which evokes a confident response. At times the teaching is brilliant. The standards achieved are appropriate to the individual abilities of the pupils, who have plenty of opportunities to work on their own in a variety of group situations. The confidence, poise and awareness of the older girls make a great impression and the school appears to be eminently successful in its aim of preparing them for the adult world

The sample

All these schools were considered to be achieving a measure of success well above the average. They differ in legal status, in organisational type, in geographical location, in the level of ability and social background of their intake, in their history and traditions, in the quality of their buildings and equipment, in their standards of staffing and in their academic achievements. Two things distinguish them from the average. First, their success in achieving a match between the ability and aptitudes of their pupils and the academic and social standards they attain; between their resources and the programmes realistically devised to exploit them; and between their potential for service to home and community and its realisation. Second, the extent to which they display quality over a number of aspects in their life and work. No one should expect perfection, and these schools would readily admit to weaknesses; but they keep their progress under critical review and where they are aware of weaknesses they are at pains to try to eradicate them.

The enquiry strengthend the view that 'success' can be attributed, in part at least, to the quality achieved in those aspects of a school's life and work isolated in this survey and examined and exemplified in the sections which follow.

2   Fundamental Objectives

Most schools would wish to claim that they had fundamental and broad objectives that were not lost to sight in the effort to attain more immediate results in the examination room or on the games field. The schools chosen proposed such broad aims as the establishment of good relationships and tension-free discipline; the development of self-confidence and self-respect; the acquisition of knowledge and skills in terms of literacy, numeracy, aesthetic sensibility and physical well-being; the perception through the curriculum of social, moral and religious values and standards for healthy living—and all these things in a context which takes account of what has gone before at the primary stage and, through careers education, what is to come in the world of work or continued education.

It is easy to pay lip-service to such high-sounding ideals. What is impressive about the schools in the sample is the ways in which they seek to achieve them by deliberate planning.

Good relationships are characteristic of them all. In the small direct grant school the headmaster knows every boy by his Christian name; in the larger Church of England comprehensive school the headmaster and senior mistress know not only the children's surnames but also significant factors in their home backgrounds—particularly valuable in an area in which there is a high proportion of broken homes. In these two schools the senior staff had deliberately timetabled themselves to teach the whole of the first year.

In the much larger schools it is not possible for the heads to know every child but they take great pains to establish structures of co-operation and discipline that foster good relationships. The headmaster of the comprehensive in the educational priority area emphasised that true mutual respect and consideration for others, in a sympathetic and well-ordered community, were the only basis for good relationships: merely to emphasise conformity with superficial standards of dress and speech would be to court rejection of them (as adult and middle class) by young people in that environment. In every example, discipline appears to be natural, and mutual respect is revealed in the casual courtesies of adults and pupils meeting in corridors as well as in good order in classrooms. The young people respond to the efforts of the staffs and take advantage of the many opportunities offered to them in and out of school. In the large comprehensive in an industrial setting, the headmaster said, "Discipline is often old fashioned as well as modern. Respect is sought, individuals are treated as such, but all misdeeds are punished. Staff and pupils know exactly the context in which they work, what is expected and what are the limits. The aim is to be the wise and sympathetic parent who does not shrink from what has to be done." This combination of firmness and understanding appears to have its effect in time: in another school one fourth form which previously had had a very bad record of truancy, aggravated by parental non-cooperation, achieved a steadier attendance.

The schools with a non-selective intake avowedly set themselves to secure the maximum development of each individual, no matter what his level of ability. Most of them have a fully-developed system of collaboration with feeder primary schools and with the parents of new entrants so that some measure of continuity is secured between primary and secondary stages, and pupils have at least a nodding acquaintance with the staff who will teach them and the buildings to which they are transferring. Moreover, and most importantly, parents understand the aims and policies of the secondary school. Several produce a brochure which gives relevant facts and a warm and friendly welcome: one, produced by a city school, begins: "We welcome your child into the school and hope that he will start in a spirit of pleasurable anticipation and confident purpose".

In all the schools much thought has been given to pastoral and academic organisation and to courses of study to ensure that each child matters, and to secure for each a consciousness of at least a measure of success. Schools are alive to the dangers of labelling children, and in no school in the survey is the academic organisation based on streaming. On the contrary, many have adopted policies of mixed-ability grouping at least in the lower forms. These matters are returned to in a later section.

In general, the curricula of the schools fall into the traditional subject pattern, though there are significant exceptions and a fairly widespread preference for some integration of subjects for younger pupils. But all the schools accept as relevant the challenge of evaluating curricula in terms of numeracy, literacy, aesthetic sensibility and physical and spiritual well-being. They are well aware of the need to develop skills as well as to amass knowledge, though for some it is more novel to think of evaluating work in terms of the development of critical faculties. But the direct grant school is already skilled in exploiting the resources of the City Library on its doorstep to encourage project work. One eleven-year-old had undertaken a genuine piece of research into the reading of 5 to 7 year-olds, interviewing children in their primary school and analysing the books they read by types and authors: the Children's Librarian was proud to receive a copy of his 'thesis'! This is admittedly an exceptional case, but a school is responsible for recognising the potential of the most gifted and for providing them with challenging opportunities.

All these schools are concerned that the study of subjects should lead to an awareness of values and they could indicate sections of syllabuses where the aim is explicit. Health education is particularly emphasised in the voluntary comprehensive school where it is a timetabled subject for the third, fourth and fifth years and is taken by a team of teachers for each year group, assisted by outside speakers. This successful course comprises lectures to a whole year group, instruction in class, and discussion in small groups of about 14 pupils: it appeared to be much enjoyed and appreciated.

The world beyond school and its importance to the individual are by no means overlooked in the definition of broad educational objectives: all the schools which had older pupils not only provide examination courses for entry to further education but also, through careers education and community service, bring young people into fruitful contact with the outside world.

Personal competence and preparation for life are perhaps the keynotes of the special school included in the sample. Examinations are totally irrelevant but the older girls can discuss problems of morals, religion, health and society in a purposeful, dignified and unselfconscious way. Broad educational objectives are as important to them as to the academically brilliant and their poise, social awareness and preparedness for the adult world of work bear testimony to the appropriateness of the objectives and the success of the school in achieving them.

3 Pastoral Care and Oversight of Academic Progress

All the schools visited have effective systems for pastoral care and for the oversight of academic progress. Though the structures differ in detail, the functions, obligations and responsibilities of all members of staff are clearly known and understood (sometimes being set out in job specifications), the communications network is straightforward and reliable, and there is sufficient flexibility to avoid rigid demarcations and to cope with the unexpected. Naturally, the small schools have less need of an elaborate system than the large. But in both, the essential ingredient is the close collaboration of all members of staff: in the small school much of this can be taken for granted; in the large it requires a machinery of pastoral committees and academic boards. One such pastoral board was attended by HM Inspectors: it consisted of the head, co-ordinating tutors, the education welfare officer and a social worker. When a child was discussed the tutors could speak of his work in school and the social worker could fill in details of the home background. In a case of persistent absence the education welfare officer was able to say that the children were being prevented from coming to school by the parents and that prosecution would have to be undertaken.

In all the schools, pastoral and academic systems interlock so that an all-round view of the pupil is created. In the majority of schools visited this is achieved by giving the form master a key role and by ensuring that he has the help and support of whatever structure is necessary.

The test of a system is the degree to which each pupil and his circumstances, aspirations and development are well known to at least one teacher and the extent to which such information is readily available and used. Satisfactory evidence of this was forthcoming in all the schools in this survey: indeed, most could show that such intimate knowledge of the individual was acquired by more than one teacher.

Much thought has been given to suitable forms of record and of record keeping and to ways in which information can be readily available to those who have need of it without endangering confidentiality on reserved matters. Keeping parents informed is another aspect which is treated seriously and imaginatively. Grading by effort as well as achievement is common and the termly or biannual report is the normal method of review. One school staggers its report writing through the year not only to relieve pressure on staff but also to facilitate parent meetings by year groups immediately after the issue of reports. Another school encourages parents to write comments on the reports before returning them to school. All the schools expect parents to visit to discuss their child's progress and they receive a good response. In one, where the system is to arrange appointments to meet tutors, two or three parents are to be found in the school every day.

Another important test of the effectiveness of a system of pastoral care is the degree to which pupils understand the system devised for their benefit and believe that their problems will receive a sympathetic hearing. In one school, interviews with small groups of boys were arranged at which such questions could be discussed with the inspectors. The answers were reassuring: the pupils knew the system and believed in it. It was particularly interesting that when they were asked to imagine themselves in a 'scrape', they responded spontaneously to the suggestion that advice and help might be forthcoming. Some thought first of their parents or their peer group; but within the school the headmaster, the chaplain, the form master, a subject master and the choir master were all suggested by different boys as the one to whom they would turn: clearly, pastoral care is no empty formality nor artificially the preserve of a single 'official'. In another large comprehensive school the staff talked about the special cases with which they had to deal. It was obvious that a difficult case of a teenager's pregnancy, for example, had been handled with humanity and understanding.

An added advantage of the time and thought given to the elaboration of successful systems of care and oversight is the degree to which such systems have knitted staffs together and given everyone an appropriate and satisfying role within a consultative framework. There is ample evidence of the altruism of staff in undertaking duties that extend far beyond their work in the classroom and the set hours of the school day; but there were also many expressions of satisfaction in the doing of it. Inevitably, the organisational side of school life is expensive of time, particularly if pastoral interviews and committee meetings are timetabled as they often need to be. In the large secondary modern school the necessarily elaborate system cost, in time devoted by some 15 senior staff to administrative and pastoral duties, the equivalent of about four full-time teachers. It was significant that in these ten schools, whose staffing ratios varied from 1:8·2 in the special school to 1:20 in the very large secondary modern school, even those which were not generously staffed made time in their programmes for adequate pastoral care. The quality of education is by no means entirely dependent on favourable staffing ratios. Nevertheless, in one school at least the weight and variety of duties bore heavily on some members of staff who showed signs of strain.

4 Curriculum Design and Academic Organisation

Pastoral care and the oversight of progress are linked naturally in these schools because they see themselves, essentially, as institutions for learning, even if, as in the case of the special school, that learning is mainly concerned with social competence. Most schools in England concerned to develop curricula appropriate to the age, ability and aptitude of their pupils interpret this not only as a matter of elaborating subject courses but also of endeavouring to take account of the whole experience of school life. As far as content is concerned, there is general agreement that, for the years of compulsory schooling, the humanities, mathematics, science, creative arts, physical and spiritual development should be the elements common to all curricula. There is general agreement, too, that within this framework there should be opportunities in the latter part of the course for options which will match career interests, preferences and the emerging abilities of the individual, provided that a degree of specialisation that would prevent choice of advanced course or career is avoided. Examination requirements are accepted as a legitimate goal at this stage, provided that they do not dominate the programme, distort the balance of the curriculum or set unrealistic targets for the student. It is commonly held that able pupils as they grow older require opportunities to study in depth, to embrace the ideals of scholarship and to become increasingly responsible for their own habits of study and their own progress. Most would declare their belief in the continuing need, at this stage, for opportunities in practical and aesthetic pursuits and for general studies: that is, for the discussion and study of broad philosophical, social and cultural questions that may not fall within the purview of an examination.

Such criteria are satisfied in the schools under review, although their solutions to the problems differ. All have given considerable time and thought to the problems of academic organisation and curriculum design. In the larger schools policy is often determined by an academic board or a curriculum committee and implemented through a departmental or faculty structure. Some had set up working parties to review organisation: in the direct grant school, for example, a small working party had marshalled all the departmental arguments in favour of a five-year course for all in preference to the existing system which promoted able boys to the sixth form after four years.

None of the schools seeks to solve the problem of matching the curriculum to ability by fine streaming, though setting in certain subjects is common. The unit of organisation in the first one, two or three years in about half the schools is the mixed ability form; in the rest, pupils are divided by ability into three broad bands. One or two schools use both patterns at different stages. In those schools which for social and educational reasons have deliberately chosen to adopt mixed ability grouping there is a critical awareness of the difficulties involved. The problem is how to individualise the teaching in ways which keep pupils at full stretch and yet provide a common starting point for all and equal opportunity to contribute to a common outcome. Much effort has been put into elaborating work sheets which take account of variations in reading ability and of general competence. Some teachers now find that this is tipping the balance towards individual work unduly and that pupils are being denied the stimulation and help that class discussion and teaching can bring, and experiment to achieve the right balance continues.

All the non-selective schools experiment with different kinds of organisation and different teaching methods for slow learners; they are constantly assessing the effects of their experiments. It is recognised that remedial departments have the disadvantage of removing the less able from the company of their contemporaries for too much of the week even though the work of the remedial class can be more easily integrated and designed to meet their needs exclusively. On the other hand a system of withdrawing the less able from normal classes, while it can help to remedy specific weaknesses of backward children, can provide too little support for the dull or severely retarded who on return to their normal class tend to flounder. Once again, the search is for a proper balance in provision.

Some schools superimpose on their form organisation a grouping into lower, middle and upper schools so as to create more homogeneous age groups with which the pupils can identify and within which broad educational aims can be seen and followed more obviously. The school in split premises has endeavoured to turn the division to advantage by giving the lower section a senior master and mistress of its own and a freedom to develop its own ethos and ways of working.

In general, the first three years have a common curriculum and all the schools ensure that creative subjects are given a fair proportion of time throughout. One comprehensive school in a poor area is well satisfied with its traditional organisation and curriculum. The common course comprises the traditional subjects, there is no experiment in integrated studies, and innovations such as computer studies and control technology are left to a later stage. The policy of the headmaster is to make haste slowly in order to carry parents, pupils and staff along at a pace they can tolerate. He would like to experiment with combined studies and with new patterns of teacher co-operation because he believes that the curriculum might gain in meaning and richness and the teaching in variety and quality. But by innovating judiciously, he tempers idealism and ambition with realism and common sense: the curriculum suits the pupils because it matches their expectations. The junior high school also sees its function in terms of building sound foundations through a common curriculum for all its pupils: "The high school's function is to provide a broad, general, liberalising education which will serve as a foundation for the more specialised work in the upper school. We have accordingly tried to meet our pupils' learning potential by a challenging curriculum, embracing a full range of subjects, with a time allocation common to all three years."

But innovation is not lacking and has been greatly facilitated by the importance attached to regular departmental consultation. In many of the schools in the sample departmental or faculty meetings are timetabled weekly. Some schools have set up working parties on curriculum development; others have encouraged innovation within subject areas by block timetabling. This appears to be having a beneficial effect on learning and teaching since the choice of activity and the time given to it are more easily varied and the grouping of pupils and staff is more flexible. A large comprehensive school has adopted a faculty rather than a subject structure and the curriculum is conceived in terms of five broad areas: science and mathematics; English and modern languages; creative studies, social studies, and religious education; physical education; and careers education. Some of the schools are also experimenting with integrated studies: humanities courses which embrace English, history, geography and religious studies are common. In one school the course in humanities is a common course taken by all fourth formers. It is not only good in itself but, introduced at this stage for all pupils, it has been found to have a valuable unifying effect on the school. Other integrated courses encountered included environmental science (a first year course in science and geography) and the making of the landscape (a fourth and fifth year course in history and geography). A very interesting and successful example of an integrated course is outdoor education, a course for second-year pupils at the direct grant school which is a hybrid of environmental studies and outdoor physical training. Joint planning with a university department of education means that four university staff and 12 postgraduate students are available to assist the school staff. Six groups of ten pupils have each the help of two university students and a member of staff. One half day a week is given to field study and the aim of the course is to discover by personal observation what use man has made of the local river valley from its source to its mouth. The disciplines brought to bear include mathematics, physics, chemistry and biology, history, geography, geology and English. School syllabuses in these subjects are adapted to take account of and prepare for the possibilities of field work. Each week the pupils produce written work arising from the topic and at the end of the year submit an individual project. In the field, pupils receive training in orienteering, canoeing, pony trekking, walking and camping. The scheme has proved so successful that its extension to the third year is under consideration.

Another example of the way in which traditional subjects can be made more exciting to youngsters is the technical

activities course in the independent school included in the
sample. A beginning is made in the third year as part of a
timetabled, rotational course in practical activities; thereafter
it flourishes as a voluntary club activity. The aim is to encourage the pupils to identify their need for knowledge and
skill arising from a technological project, to investigate and
study their problems, to apply what they learn to the construction of their model and then to evaluate their results. Beginning
with simple tasks of building a power-controlled model boat
or aircraft, the boys later design their own projects such as
radio-controlled model vehicles, ships and aircraft, a self-con-
trolling solar heating dish, a hovercraft, tracked vehicles and
electronic timing devices for photography. Some 48 different
projects were under construction at the time of the visit to the
school and much of the work seen was of outstanding ingenuity
and quality. The scheme patently develops a high degree of
creative ability and an attitude of enquiry and investigation; it
amply fulfils the school's broad aim of "encouraging self-
expression and self-realisation through creative activity".

An unusual example of integrated studies is the course at
the same school which is labelled 'predicament, experiment and
belief' and which extends through the first three years. Its object
is to present to younger boys an integrated view of man in his
physical environment in the past and present and of the
religious beliefs whereby he gives meaning to his experience.
The emphasis is on understanding the techniques of study in
the disciplines involved rather than on amassing factual knowledge. The course has been in operation for nine years and is
constantly revised. The staff involved meet for planning sessions
weekly and they have built up a considerable range of resources,
including books to support the work. The interests of the pupils
is lively, the approach is scholarly and the work produced has
significance and quality.

Curriculum choice at the fourth year stage is, as in most
schools, a common feature. What is particularly interesting is
the width of choice offered and the careful planning and
guidance that ensures that a pupil's curriculum remains coherent
and balanced. Schools without a generous staffing ratio man-
aged to offer choices from combinations of subjects in such a
way that other sections of the school were not unduly robbed
of man-power. Planning is also imaginative for the less able or
less well-motivated pupil. The modern school with 1,350 pupils
on roll, for example, offers a guided choice of five subjects
from five combinations totalling 60 courses which are added to
the common core of religious education, English, mathematics,
physical education and citizenship. Everyone has to take science
but the course may be general science, physical science, biology,
chemistry or human biology. New subjects such as community
work projects, motor vehicle engineering or parentcraft are introduced to tempt the less academically interested to renewed
effort. The large comprehensive school which regards its policy
as a traditional one places pupils at this stage in three bands:
those taking GCE or CSE examinations in a choice of 20 sub-

jects; those taking CSE only, with 19 subjects offered; and, for the less able, an integrated course. The last provides a choice of 13 subjects and includes studies such as computer science, and home-making together with a common core of English, mathematics, social studies and science all linked in the study of common themes such as 'war and society'. Health, careers and physical education are compulsory and taught separately to these pupils.

The problem of providing for the less able or the poorly motivated is acute for the large 13 to 18 school in a depressed area in northern England. An outward-looking course is being developed, called the 'school-based course', which has no set syllabus but involves local visits and work experience followed by a variety of work in school, arising from what the pupils have seen and done. Originally it was designed for one day a week, but its success is such that next year it will operate on every day of the week. In addition, the school has made special arrangements for the small group of pupils whose learning and behavioural problems have proved exceptionally difficult to cope with in the normal classroom situation. They are based on the house in the school grounds, and when not following (in school) those courses in which they have shown interest and readiness to work, they undertake activities in the school house and grounds such as gardening, cookery, typing or light craft. They were supervised by the headmaster and some senior teachers but a full-time warden (previously a youth tutor) has now been installed in a flat in the house and he has taken charge of these boys and girls. He visits their homes and encourages their parents to visit the school house; he works closely with the careers officer who specialises in the placement of the less able; and his wife (although not officially employed) makes a significant contribution. She is often able to establish a non-authoritarian relationship with the young people and has been known to offer a night's lodging and a 'cooling-off' period for those at loggerheads with their parents. It is not surprising to find that some boys and girls return to the house in the evening and at weekends to finish tasks that they have started during the day and that former pupils often visit the warden and his wife—sometimes with their girl or boy friends.

The schools with sixth forms of able pupils working for GCE advanced levels offer a wide range of subjects and timetable in such a way that combinations of arts and science subjects are possible. One example of a sixth form of 120 pupils studying 17 A-level subjects in 76 different combinations is typical of those schools with large sixth forms and a long tradition of advanced work. All give serious attention to general studies. One programme provides for religious education, the use of English and the BBC programmes, 'Prospect' and 'New Horizons', together with six units of study spread over two years. At present these comprise courses in the language of mathematics, the ideas of science, the uses of literacy, introduction to sociology, the heritage of western civilisation, and government and law.

Comprehensive schools are finding that they must provide not only for the academically able but also for the 'new sixth formers'—those who want to stay on but are unable or do not wish to follow traditional advanced courses. One school in the sample has devised a self-contained one-year course for them. It comprises a school-based element covering six subject areas together with link courses taken at two local colleges of further education which offer units on 'service in the community', 'business studies' and 'community studies'. Most of the courses, including those at the technical colleges, are assessed by the examinations for the experimental Certificate of Extended Education proposed by the Schools Council.

A new problem for secondary schools is how to hold young people at school in their last term of attendance after public examinations are over. It is an indication of the quality of the large secondary modern school included in the survey that, despite the fact that in a seaside town in summer temporary employment is easy to find, a special six-week, post CSE course has gained an 80 per cent response. Thirty-three members of staff were involved in mounting a great variety of optional courses, mainly in practical or leisure pursuits, and all the pupils had the chance of a residential course or of camping. The problem also affects, though less acutely, those students who intend to continue their education after the fifth year. One school keeps them interested in the post-examination period by providing 'taster' courses or sixth-form studies which also enable them to make informed choices of the advanced courses they will later follow.

Staff and Quality of Work

It is a commonplace that a school will be as good as the quality of its staff and the quality of their team work. It is a feature of all these schools that much attention has been given to departmental or faculty organisation and that the staff spend a considerable amount of time in planning and discussing their courses and their teaching. In some schools provision is made in the timetable for departmental planning, and this would seem to be a wise investment: but what requires to be done if the staff work in teams, pool their ideas on aims, method and content, and regularly evaluate their success in achieving objectives cannot all be encompassed within school hours. In a number of other schools, innovations in the curriculum and integrated courses which often involved team teaching increased the necessity for close collaboration. The reward is a clarity of aim and a uniformity of purpose, far above the average, that lifts the general standard of effectiveness in the classroom very much higher than it would otherwise be. In the schools visited, the general level of competence, of shared understanding and purpose made for an evenness of achievement that is commendable.

Good preparation, variety of approach, regular and constructive correction of pupils' work and consistent encouragement are the hallmarks of successful teaching seen. One example must suffice. In the junior high school, planned departmental meetings have greatly facilitated the work of the science team who keep content and method under review, seeking to combine the best of the traditional courses with new material and methods. Demonstrations to a whole class alternate with group experiments; individuals at times work through a 'circus' of experiments on a common theme; practical work is followed up by directed reading in the resources area. Abler pupils have special assignments and one group was seen investigating plant growth, using sophisticated experimental techniques. There is good oral work at all times and the emphasis throughout is on understanding and on genuine scientific method. Enough has been said earlier on innovation in the curriculum to indicate that many of the schools are reacting imaginatively to the demands of their situation and are well aware of current ideas of curriculum development: but the teachers are wise enough to keep new practices under critical review, to proceed at a pace that is appropriate to them, to their individual pupils and to parental understanding and to resist the temptation to adopt every change of fashion.

An analysis of the staffing of these ten schools shows that the initial qualifications of teachers, their length of experience or their years of service to a school are not necessarily prime factors in a school's success. Some, like the independent and direct grant schools, are staffed almost completely by graduates. The special school has no graduates, but all staff have had special training in addition to their certificate course. Other schools, like the small voluntary-aided comprehensive, have 80 per cent graduates; but the large secondary modern has far fewer, though all have had professional training. In the rest, graduates and non-graduates in about equal proportions are employed. Nor is professional experience alone a sufficient factor: about half the teachers in all these schools are under 30 and very few are over 50. Finally, it has already been said that team work and common purpose characterise these schools: but this was not necessarily the outcome of a partnership spread over a long period. More than half the teachers had served in their particular school for less than five years: in one large comprehensive, no fewer than 73 out of a total of 96 had been appointed within the last five years, and of the 87 appointments made in the last four years 63 had been of probationers. Willingness to tackle the task, readiness to plan and work with colleagues and to pool ideas, and leadership which rapidly establishes an esprit de corps and common objectives, understood and pursued by all, appear to be much more important factors in securing success than the level of initial qualifications, experience or continuity of service.

A test of the quality of staffing is undoubtedly the support that is provided for the new entrant to the profession. These schools, formally and informally, take care of their probationers, assign them work within their powers and involve them in team organisations and policy decisions. The direct grant school has gone further and in collaboration with the university department of education and heads of other city schools has pioneered a scheme of induction and training for all the probationers of the area.

It is not unreasonable to regard measurable results as one test of the quality of teaching and where examinations are appropriate to the pupils it is to be expected that a school of quality will achieve results that are better than average. But schools are not to be judged by examination results alone. The special school, for example, takes no examinations, but the work is well above average and few pupils appear to be underachieving. What they do forms a good foundation for entry into employment and for stability in life: the poise and social awareness of the senior girls is outstanding. The junior high school is also free of external examinations but this does not mean that it can ignore the requirements of the next stage: nor does it do so. For the rest, the schools included in the sample are achieving results in external examinations that, in general, are well above average. A number have married examination requirements and their own views of content and approach by devising Mode 3 courses for the CSE; the independent school has done the same in English for both the ordinary and the advanced levels of the GCE. The voluntary aided comprehensive school has, in the minimum time, built up a sixth form of 100 pupils who originally had not been selected for grammar school education. The two comprehensive schools in the north of England have adopted a realistic view of the abilities and expectations of their pupils and have resisted the temptation to be over-ambitious in developing advanced academic work. The independent and direct grant schools have consistently attained outstanding results over a wide range of subjects at the highest levels. To generalise, the successful school encourages individual pupils to attain the highest standard of which they are capable by providing an appropriate challenge.

6 Premises and Resources and their Use

Good premises do not make a good school, but if they are to be adequate for their purpose premises must reach minimum standards. In only one example does provision fall below the minimum required: the direct grant school, through lack of workshops, cannot include heavy craft in its curriculum. Its buildings are inconvenient and its site substandard but it has made the best of what it has; as it lies in the shadow of a cathedral it has an incomparable setting for school assemblies. In contrast, the small special school is established in a beautiful 18th century house set in extensive grounds and well maintained gardens, and the modern extensions to the mansion have not detracted from its beauty. Two other schools are a mixture of old and new: the independent school combines 18th Century Palladian and 20th Century Contemporary: the comprehensive in the mining area combines a distinguished mansion and new blocks in CLASP. The large secondary modern school comprises two former schools and thus operates on a split site. For the rest, the schools visited have, with one exception, been built or extended within the last ten years.

Not all the problems of accommodation have been solved and most schools are in need of more small rooms for departmental headquarters and tutorial spaces or of better arrangements of suites of classrooms and activity areas for major subjects. The staff of one school had been consulted on the design of an additional area for teaching English and the humanities. The planning made possible the style of teaching that the school wished to adopt and the accommodation consists of carpeted spaces capable of flexible arrangement, well placed in relation to the library and resources centre, and a study area equipped with carrels. For others, the addition of fifth or sixth form centres has provided appropriately for the scope and style of a developing curriculum. Most of the schools, but not all, are alive to the possibilities of creating their own atmosphere by tasteful and interesting displays in classrooms and circulation areas. All take pride in their buildings, new or old, and keep them tidy, clean and orderly. Time and use had in some instances made buildings more attractive rather than less. The harsh newness of brick and concrete of the comprehensive school in the working class district of an industrial city had mellowed after eight years: stark walls are draped by creepers and roadways adorned with hanging baskets and well kept flower beds. The pupils have played their part and the interior has a civilised air with its interesting displays and remarkable cleanliness.

Resources in these schools are, in general, adequate and sometimes impressive. The junior high school, opened in splendid buildings in 1968, has the distinction of possessing its own nature trail in its grounds. The direct grant school has the City Library on its doorstep. The independent school has two libraries with a stock of 14,000 books which are about to be rehoused in a new building. But it is not only the ancient foundations that can boast of their libraries: the large secondary modern also has 14,000 volumes and generous loan collections from the County library; the comprehensive school in the mining area has been able to adapt the assembly hall of its original building as a library of splendid proportions. To exploit it, it has been wise enough to give the teacher-librarian both clerical assistance and a light teaching timetable of no more than ten periods a week. A number of schools are extending their non-book stock and developing resource centres, particularly in order to support the teaching of classes of mixed abilities. Most schools are reasonably well equipped with audio-visual aids. The small secondary modern school, in particular, makes excellent use of them. This school is also noteworthy for the great variety of animals that are housed, indoors and out, in cages and sheds made by the boys. The livestock is aptly used in the teaching; that the animals are also very well cared for and cherished is an indication of the quality of outlook of the school as a whole.

Links with the Local Community

With so much to recommend these schools it was not surprising to find that the pupils had a proper pride in them and that they are held in esteem locally. The large neighbourhood school in a depressed industrial area now finds, in fact, that a good number of parents in other parts of the city select this school as their first choice and though six local primary schools contribute two-thirds of the annual intake small groups of pupils come from about 30 other primary schools.

All the schools are at pains to develop close links with parents. A number have produced brochures which give information about the school and an outline of its aims and courses. All make special arrangements to welcome newcomers and their parents. Heads are sensitive to the wishes and expectations of parents and take them into account in their planning, if need be adjusting the pace of change in areas where parents are suspicious of innovation. Information on pupils' progress is regularly supplied both formally and informally. One school, at least, keeps primary schools in touch with the progress of their former pupils. All have given careful thought to the type of report that will be helpful to parents and normally seek to expand the information by interviews. In poorer areas there is an impressive amount of home visiting either by school staff, youth tutors or school nurses. Parent-teacher organisations are commonplace. The voluntary aided school has introduced a Family Eucharist conducted by the chairman of governors, the rural dean, as an expression of what the school stands for. Communion was taken by parents, teachers, pupils, governors and other friends of the school, many of whom assisted in the service.

In many cases, the contribution that the school is making to the local community is considerable. Buildings are often used for adult classes: in the independent school, on Saturday mornings, parents can join with boys, either as teachers or as the taught, in a variety of cultural, social and athletic activities. The comprehensive school in the mining town is to all intents a community school: a youth club under a member of staff is held on the premises; the sixth form have a Friday evening club (their unit being available to them on other evenings for study purposes). Those responsible for further education in the area co-operate closely with the school and full use is made of the school premises each evening and at weekends for vocational and non-vocational classes and general leisure activities. Another comprehensive school is planning joint use by school and community of its physical education facilities and sports centre.

Specific service to the community is frequently included in school courses. One school has planned a six-months optional course in social service which is to be taken by a teacher/youth tutor; a number have schemes for helping the aged in their homes, delivering 'meals on wheels', visiting the sick in hospital, or assisting in play groups. Another school is making a survey of local derelict land and undertaking work, such as painting a church hall or railings, requested by the community; one has a wind band and another a military band which play in hospitals and give concerts locally. The direct grant school has an ambitious theatre tour organised to take three plays to a seaside town with a cast drawn from among its own boys and from the girls of a neighbouring school. The independent school makes community service a compulsory course for one term and thereafter provides continued opportunities for voluntary work. The administration and financing of projects are in the hands of the boys themselves and on Thursday afternoons as many as 200 boys can be engaged on this course. At the time of the visit, about 60 per cent of them were busy out of school, helping old people, giving games coaching at primary schools, teaching slow readers or taking the handicapped shopping, sailing or riding.

Schools are alive to the need for close links with the social services, and in many the educational welfare officer, the school nurse and local social workers are frequent visitors. Contact with the police is often actively fostered and in one school they came not only to give specialist demonstrations but also to participate in sporting activities with the boys.

Many schools touch a wider community through their international contacts and exchange visits. The independent school has its international centre, others arrange exchanges with France and Germany.

Careers guidance is an accepted part of pastoral care in all the schools visited and the help of the Careers Advisory Service is valued: in one example the Careers Officer has his office in the school. In some schools careers guidance has been widened to become careers education so that vocational interests are taken into account in the curriculum and opportunities for works experience provided. A distinctive feature of the work in one school (where about 70 per cent of leavers go on to universities) is the use of aptitude tests in the fifth form and of careers advisory panels, largely constituted from parents. A key factor in the scope and success of provision for careers education is the amount of time provided for the responsible teacher: at one end of the scale no more than three periods a week is provided; at the other, as many as 30 and this in a school only half the size of the other example.

8 'Climate' and Leadership

The schools visited differ in very many respects as institutions, although each can demonstrate its quality in its aims, in oversight of pupils, in curriculum design, in standards of teaching and academic achievements and in its links with the local community. What they all have in common is effective leadership and a 'climate' that is conducive to growth. The schools see themselves as places designed for learning; they take trouble to make their philosophies explicit for themselves and to explain them to parents and pupils; the foundation of their work and corporate life is an acceptance of shared values.

Emphasis is laid on consultation, team work and participation, but, without exception, the most important single factor in the success of these schools is the quality of leadership of the head. Without exception, the heads have qualities of imagination and vision, tempered by realism, which have enabled them to sum up not only their present situation but also attainable future goals. They appreciate the need for specific educational aims, both social and intellectual, and have the capacity to communicate these to staff, pupils and parents, to win their assent and to put their own policies into practice. Their sympathetic understanding of staff and pupils, their accessibility, good humour and sense of proportion and their dedication to their task has won them the respect of parents, teachers and taught. They are conscious of the corruption of power and though ready to take final responsibility they have made power-sharing the keynote of their organisation and administration. Such leadership is crucial for success and these schools are what their heads and staffs have made them.

Printed in England for Her Majesty's Stationery Office
by Burrup, Mathieson & Co., Ltd.   S256509 LE
Dd585890   K40   3/77